Couples T

A Survival Guide On How To Reconnect With Your Partner Through Honest Communication, Overcome The Anxiety In Relationship And Build A Strong Emotional Bond

John T. Collins PsyD & Rachel Collins MD

Table Of Contents

Introduction

It feels so good to say and to hear the words "I love you," but what do they really mean? In order to talk about what makes a relationship successful, it is important to have a working definition of love and understand why we choose the people we love. True and lasting love is about developing a solid, loving base supporting each other's attachment needs and giving each other mutual care. It is also about personal growth, following your own dreams and desires, and celebrating and supporting your partner in growing and actualizing their dreams and desires as well.

Every person is different and thus every relationship is different. Every relationship has different needs and expectations that are based on each partner's ability to compromise and actually be in a long-term relationship with his significant other. Admittedly you are going to marry the one you want to spend the rest of your life with and you propose to make your marriage last forever, not to get divorced. Many experts agree on several characteristics that a long-term healthy relationship has and will later lead to a solid marriage. However, keep in mind that those characteristics should not cease to exist after you have taken the vows. You still are in a relationship.

Chapter 1.   Discover Your Love Language

To discover your love language, you need to observe and be keen on the way your partner expresses his or her love to you. Take note of what you are always complaining that he or she does wrong and what he does that you like. By analyzing both situations, you get to discover your love language. Chapman also expressed that a person shows love in a way he or she would love to receive it. We all appreciate it when our partners use all the five languages; however, on most occasions, you feel more loved when they focus on your specific love language.

Words of Affirmation

It takes time to get to know a person in a relationship. As time goes by, you both get to know what your partner's likes and dislikes are. Eventually, we would all like our partners to know what ticks you off and how to respond well to it. If you like when your partner expresses love through spoken affection, praises, compliments or reassurance, then words of affirmation could just be your love language.

- **Words of appreciation**

Here you can express love by appreciating the good qualities of your partner.

- **Words of acknowledgment**

Here you can express love by recognizing the true features of your significant other.

- **Words of empathy**

You can use words to understand and share the feelings of your partner.

- **Words of admiration**

Here you can express love by showing respect and warm approval. You can say things like I really admire your jovial personality, I love how you pay close attention to, or I was impressed when you did, etc.

- **Words of encouragement**

You can use words to show support, hope, or confidence.

- **Words of humility**

You can use words to show modesty, remorse, forgiveness, and understanding.

People can express words of affirmation through spoken word, text, email, letters, and love notes. Writing love notes and leaving them on the mirror, bedside, pillow, kitchen counter or fridge, especially if you are always up before your partner, is a great idea. This is a great way to make your partner feel special and appreciated. On the flip side, people whose primary language are words of affirmation, tend to hurt more when the words change from love to hate, insults and negative comments because to them verbal cues matter a lot more.

15

Gifts

We all express and feel love differently. We do not always communicate in a way our partners respond best to because couples rarely share the same love language. However, if you love receiving gifts, giving gifts, and are always touched by the effort people put behind gift-giving, then your primary love language might just be receiving gifts.

• **The intention**

When giving a gift, it is important to have the right intention. People buy gifts to show gratitude, appreciation, remorse, or to celebrate the other person. You are not supposed to buy a gift to gain a certain benefit or to cover up for a past failure. If the intention is wrong, then the gift will not be received well.

• **Value**

Sometimes people believe in order for their gifts to be appreciated, they need to have a high price tag. The value of a gift should not be important; what matters are the sentiments tied to it. The receiver might only consider the cost of the gift when they know you cannot afford it.

- **Timing**

When giving a gift, it is important to ensure that the timing is right. A person may not appreciate a luxurious car when they are about to be evicted from their apartment or have financial difficulty. They would rather have that money to sort out their most pressing needs first.

- **The method of gift-giving**

Sometimes how the gift is given matters more than the gift. Some people feel loved when they are surprised or when the gift is accompanied by an act of service, for example, taking one for dinner then gifting them. You might have the best gift, but if it is not given well, the recipient might not appreciate it. Remember, it is not only about the gift but also about the excitement you have in giving it.

- **Gifts are not always tangible**

A person whose love language is gifting might not necessarily love something wrapped. It is important to understand that gifts are not only bought, but they can also be made or experienced. For example, a gift can be an unforgettable experience, like taking a trip or going out for adventurous activities.

- **Gift of self**

Another powerful gift of love you can give your partner is the gift of physical presence, especially if he or she is going through a hard time. Giving someone your time and attention sometimes is better than a physical gift.

- **Effort behind it**

Sometimes people give gifts for the sake of giving or because they are obligated to. Gift receivers will not be enthusiastic or feel loved about a gift if they see no effort was made when selecting the gift. If the gift is not something they need or would have bought for themselves, then they might not receive it well.

Acts of Service

People whose primary love language is acts of service feel most loved when their partners render a service or services. If you prefer someone showing you love as opposed to hearing love affirmations, then your love language is acts of service. You enjoy hearing words like "how can I help you?" more than "I love you."

Acts of service are a labor of love; however, there are three truths behind it:

• Not all acts of service are chores related - we all love to hate house chores; however, acts of service do not all revolve around house chores. Acts of service come in many forms, treating someone to a massage is an act of service

• People should not use acts of service to cover for guilt or resentment. The acts should be done out of love without conditions or expectations.

• Receivers of the acts of service would want some assistance but will never ask for it simply because they do not want to seem to be demanding. It is always better to perform an act without having them ask you to do so.

Couple in relationships whom either one or both value acts of service should not overlook whatever act of service their partners do for them no matter how small. Sometimes your partner might be performing an act of service without you even knowing it. Learn to recognize even the small things your partners do for you and appreciate them. This ensures that they do not feel like they are taking them for granted.

Quality Time

When you want nothing else from your partner other than their undivided attention, you love language might be quality time. You feel most loved when you spend quality time with your partner and unloved when he or she does not give you time. Quality time might be the easiest language to understand, but it is also misinterpreted.

If you are always complaining that your spouse does not spend enough time with you or we used to this and that together now we do not, then your love language is quality time. Quality time means giving your partner undivided attention.

People share quality time through the following:

- **By being deliberate**

People whose primary love language is quality time may not appreciate when you only want to spend time spontaneously, or last minute, they feel loved when their significant others consciously and intentionally plan for quality time together.

- **By being mentally present**

You may plan to spend quality time with your partner, but when you get to actually spending the time, you are not mentally present.

- **By being affectionate**

You can spend time with someone and be mentally present, but if you are not affectionate, your partner might not see it as time well spent.

When spending time with your partner, a spouse should ensure the following:

- He or she makes eye contact when communicating with their partner

- Avoid multitasking when communicating

- Consider your spouse's feelings

- Listen actively

Physical Touch

Many people assume that their love language is physical touch because it is a big part of any relationship; however, this is not the case. People who speak this love language feel most loved when their significant others offer physical touch. It does not have to be over the top PDA; their physical touch is about intimacy; it could be laying your head on your spouse's shoulder, running your hands through their hair, hugging, or just holding hands.

Practice the following:

- **Give Hugs**

Even though people are different in terms of the type of touch they prefer, hugs usually do the trick for most. Hugs can be given anytime and anywhere. They make the other person feel secure, comforted, and loved.

- **Handholding**

Handholding is another simple way to show physical touch; you can take your partner's hand and squeeze it between both your hands when out in public and just hold hands when taking neighborhood walks.

- **Give high fives and fist bump**

If you are not a touchy-feely person, a simple way to demonstrate love to a partner who is by giving high fives or fist pumps, especially when celebrating.

- **Back rubs**

Back rubs give a calming effect. If you notice your partner enjoys them, try to rub his or her back or neck often. Rubs can even be done in public; you can run your hand on your partner's hair while conversing with others on social gatherings. This keeps a steady stream of love.

- **Kiss their cheek or forehead**

Kissing your partner's cheek or forehead can be used as a form of greeting. You can show physical touch by kissing them when saying hello or goodbye.

- **Hold them close**

People whose primary love language is physical touch prefer to be held when they are going through a difficult time. It is a way of showing love and consoling them through hard times.

- **Dancing together**

Another way you can show love through touch is by dancing with your spouse. When you on a night out, concert, at home or attend a party, dance with each other. Dance to the hype songs and to the slow songs.

- **Make it a habit**

Make the simple acts of physical touch a habit. Always ensure you choose an appropriate time to show affection. Your partner may not want to hold hands when they are mad at you.

It is important to learn your love language and that of your partner to meet each other's emotional needs. Think about how you both like to give and receive love and what makes you feel most loved and cared for to discover your primary love languages.

Chapter 2.   Habits to Revive the Love

So, you are sure that you've found the best possible partner ever and wish to take your relationship to its next phase? Or maybe your partner wants marriage and you're not yet ready. How can you communicate this to your partner without hurting? How do you tell them that you need more time without inconsiderate or insensitive? How do you raise the topic of marriage without appearing pushy?

If you've been going around for a while, it is natural to think that it is time to take the relationship ahead. You want to pop the big question, but you are also unsure about your partner's reaction. Or maybe you are caught off guard after your partner pops the marriage question. There are several questions in your mind, including where is the relationship headed? Is it a long-term relationship? Is your partner truly the "one?"

Do you imagine yourself spending the rest of your life with him or her? You are serious with a person and wondering how to make things move ahead with them. How do you raise the topic of marriage? The most important thing is to match your goals and intentions in the long run.

Tips for Discussing Marriage or Taking Your Relationship Serious.

Be Straightforward

When you are talking about taking your relationship to the next level or suggesting marriage, keep it simple and straightforward. All the same, make your conversation low pressure. You can say something such as, "I know I want to get married in future. How do you feel about the same? You are keeping it open-ended and non-accusatory and aren't accompanying the idea by pressure.

Avoid statements such as, "Are you ever going to get married?" or "Are you planning to marry me before I die?" or "what are we really?" Approach this topic pretty much like other challenging and tricky topics with loads of maturity and positivity. You and your partner may not necessarily be on the same page when it comes to a topic as sensitive as marriage. He or she may just not be ready. You should respect that instead of putting pressure on them and making them feel miserable about their choice.

When a person says, "not now" or "they aren't ready yet," it doesn't mean never. It just means they need more time. Give them the time and space to sort out their priorities and responsibilities.

Use a General and Gentle Approach

If you get freaked out trying a straightforward or pointed approach, use a general conversation approach. Say, for example, you have a friend who got married recently. Very smoothly yet casually draw this into a conversation with your partner. If nothing, you'll be able to determine their interest in getting married or at least know their views on marriage. This move works especially well if you have a slight hint that your partner may have negative views or feelings about marriage, and you wish to avoid a potentially awkward and disappointing forthright conversation.

Approach the conversation slowly and gently. Frame your expectation as a question and not a high-pressure expectation. For instance, ask "How do you view the future of our bond or relationship?" or "Have you considered marriage down the line?" It sounds non-threatening.

Ditch the Ultimatums

Irrespective of how you broach the topic of marriage, avoid issuing ultimatums to your partner to manipulate them into doing what you want. Yes, however frustrated you are, issuing ultimatums is akin to subtly manipulating the person into giving in to your demands. We've all done it at some point or the other in a relationship.

The underlying idea is, you really don't want to force yourself or the idea of commitment on someone isn't really keen on taking it ahead yet. Why should you have to convince someone about marrying you? Isn't it counterproductive? People should want to be with you on their own. If they don't, give them more time. There's no point selling yourself or the idea of marriage to someone who clearly doesn't feel it on their own. Honestly, I would never want to convince someone to marry me! Proposals backed by threat are the worst. They push a person in the opposite direction and make them feel like their view or opinion is not important.

Don't Make Assumptions

Alright, you both love traveling, playing golf and gorging on desserts. That doesn't mean you are on the same page when it comes to marriage. Don't automatically assume that because you have similar interests or likes, you both are destined to get married. You may not be on a similar page where commitment or marriage is concerned.

I also know of instances when couples start dating wanting marriage and then don't really feel the same way one year into the relationship, which is alright. When it comes to taking your relationship ahead or committing into a bond, talk to your partner. Instead of sitting and assuming things, have a real conversation with him or her to understand their hopes, expectations, fears and concerns.

Do not assume that you are invariably headed in the direction of the altar simply on the basis that you both love each other.

Listen Keenly

Listen to what your partner is saying. Read between the lines to understand the underlying feelings and intentions. Sometimes, your direct approach may catch them off-guard. They may something you really don't want to hear. Encourage them to express themselves honestly.

There are several reasons why people may be averse to the idea of marriage or commitment, including personal insecurities, bitter relationships or marriages in the past, childhood experiences related to their parents' bitter relationship, perceived loss of freedom, greater responsibilities and much more. Listen to the other person to understand their concerns. Even if you both want marriage, your reasons can be completely different.

For example, your partner may want marriage for practical and financial reasons since it makes sense to run a single home than two. On the other hand, your partner may want to get married because they want someone to come back and talk to. Your reasons may be practical, while your partners may be more romantic.

When you talk frankly and honestly about the idea of marriage and commitment, you'll discover diverse perspectives and expectations. Of course, if you are bringing up the subject if marriage, you will be speaking more in the beginning. However, once you realize that the other person is replying to your questions, listen. When you direct the conversation, you are preventing your partner from sharing their truest feelings. Instead of speaking honestly, they will most likely tell you what you want to hear.

The same is true for hearing something you may not like. Listen carefully to their reasoning. For example, a person may really want to marry you but they may want to be more financially secure before they take the plunge. He or she may want to get their house in place first before marrying you. If you finish the conversation without letting him/her share, you may start believing that they don't want to marry you at all, which is not the truth at all.

Eliminate the scope for misunderstanding by listening keenly to what the person is saying.

Take a Stock of Your Motives

Before you begin talking about marriage with your partner, understand your motives for getting or not getting married. Why do you want to get married or not get married? Is it for financial or personal security? Is it owing to tradition? Do you want to get married to have children? Have a good grip on your motives, intentions and desires for getting married?

This will help you have a more thoughtful or meaningful conversation with your partner. It also offers greater insight into the other person about what your underlying motives are to decide. Whether he or she agrees to what you are saying or gives in to your demand largely depends on your underlying motives, and how you communicate it to your partner.

Don't Try To Be Too Cool

We are all guilty of making this mistake, where we pretend, we don't really care when we really want something to happen. You know the drill, right? You act all cool and like you don't give a damn just to save yourself the hurt and disappointment. If these things aren't really important to you, it is all good.

However, it isn't cool to pretend to have priorities that are different from your actual priorities. It isn't really fair for either you or your partner. Honestly is the best approach when it comes to talking about marriage and commitment.

Don't Rush If You Don't Want To

Yes, marriage is a huge decision. Career wise, financially and personally! You may have legitimate reasons for not being ready for marriage yet. You may not want additional responsibility of your shoulder yet when you are still trying to find your bearings in a new job or career. Similarly, you may not be in a position to devote time to having and raring children if you are on the brink of your career.

You'll have to feel with your heart, but you'll also have to use your mind for thinking rationally about a life changing decision. Do not let your partner put you under any pressure or manipulate you into giving in to their demand. There are plenty of energy drainers in our life to add more. Don't rush. Communicate with your partner gently and assertively that you need more time. Tell them that you adore them and that it isn't about them but how you feel unprepared or need more time to come to terms with a bigger commitment. Don't focus on them; make it about your lack of readiness. At the same time, ensure they know that "not now" doesn't mean "never."

Ask your partner questions such as, "Why do you want to get married?" " Why do you want to make it happen so quickly?" "What do we gain from the marriage that we don't have already?" and other similar questions. Ask yourself if you are truly willing to spend your life with a person who is pressurizing you into making such an important issue about your life. Doesn't it reflect unflatteringly on them if they are pushing you into deciding? This may just be a teaser or trailer of things to follow. Even if your partner doesn't agree with you, he/she must respect your feelings and choices.

Be True to Yourself

Whether you want marriage or not, learn to be true to yourself. Don't go with something just because your partner is saying it or you feel compelled to agree with them. You have your own independent feelings and opinions, which should be expressed in a healthy, polite and assertive manner. Express your honest feelings about marriage. Is marriage a priority for you in the immediate future? Are you on the same thought process or plane as your partner? Don't pretend you are if you aren't.

Chapter 3.   Relationship Strengthening Activities

When it comes to relationship issues, sometimes a couple is unable to note that there is a problem that may jeopardize dynamics and functionality of their relationship until the problem becomes evolved to the point where it appears to be drawing only more problems. That is why it is likewise important to work on preventing these issues, which is most efficiently done with relationship-strengthening activities for couples. There is always more room for improvement, while your relationship should flourish as long as you are ready to try and commit.

"Pillow Talks"

We can't emphasize enough how important clear communication in relationships is. That is why our first relationship-strengthening activity on the list is dedicated to encouraging communication between couples. One of the best ways of practicing communication is to start with casual and "carefree" talk sessions. If you are used to spending the evening alone but together – you may continue to read that book you started with several days ago and your partner is hooked to the TV or smartphone – you may decide to disconnect from lonesome activities and shut off the world, while you focus on each other. You may lay down in bed or settle down on the sofa, it doesn't matter which location you choose – what matters is that you are not alone together. Start talking about your day, about your plans, start a conversation on anything that crosses your mind. Pillow talk topics may also revolve around affectionate talk, which is a great way of showing appreciation for your partner through verbal and non-verbal communication. Cuddling is also allowed as you are talking, sharing opinions and focusing on what the other has to say. This exercise is due to help you establish or reestablish connection with your partner, while practicing openness, communication, appreciation and intimacy. Once you make these "pillow talks" your and your partner's routine, you might be surprised by how many new things you and your partner have found out about your each other.

Mutual Interests and Hobbies

Although you and your partner may be different when it comes to preferences and characteristics, you surely have some things in common. In case you start tracing similarities between your partner and yourself, you may be surprised with how many things you actually have in common. Everything you and your partner have in common can be used as an advantage in the process of improving your relationship. One of the best ways of strengthening your relationship is to find activities and hobbies that suit your mutual interests and focus on connecting through these activities. Instead of focusing on the ways you are different from one another, you should place an emphasis on similarities that can serve the purpose of helping you reconnect with your partner, while taking advantage of spending more time together through shared activities and hobbies.

"Who Are You?"

In the beginning of every relationship, your partner appears to be a perfect match and everything you feel and see speaks in favor of the idea that you have found an ideal partner. As time is passing by, you are getting to know each other better, so both you and your partner are starting to notice flaws and characteristics that might get in the way of the "ideal". The fact is, there is no ideal. There is no perfection except a perfect imperfection – that means that you and your partner should be able to accept each other with flaws and traits, likewise, in case you truly love each other. As mentioned earlier in the book, acceptance, recognition and appreciation are some of the key qualities of a happy and healthy relationship. Don't be afraid to dig deeper, and don't be afraid to open yourself to your partner. One of relationship-strengthening activities that may help you improve your relationship at the very start, is getting to know each other better through a series of exercises for couples. For starters, you can exchange your favorite books, play favorite music to each other and agree to watch each other's favorite movies together. You may also get involved in quiz talk, asking your partner "trivia" questions that you believe would reveal a bit more about your partner's characteristics. For example, if you are watching a horror movie, you may ask your partner what his biggest fear is. Every shared activity with your partner is another way of getting closer to knowing each other better. By sharing your favorite books, music, movies and other personal things that your partner may be interested in, you are actually sharing a piece of your own characteristics and preferences, that way deepening intimacy and connection. Moreover, you are getting a hold of appreciation for differences and similarities that describe you as a couple.

No Dwelling Allowed

Couples fight, argue, can encounter disagreements, and tend to enter conflicts out of numerous different reasons – and as we emphasized on more than several occasions through the book, this is a perfectly normal thing in any relationship, including romantic relationships (perhaps, especially romantic relationships). Conflicts and disagreements arise as a way of testing the strength of a relationship, while failing often means not putting enough effort in resolving problems you might have with your partner. Conflicts may "pack up" to create more serious issues and may result in losing intimacy and connection you have with your partner, which furthermore may shake the very foundation of your relationship. Before you allow this to happen, you and your partner can work on preventive measures through couples' activities for strengthening. Whenever you and your partner enter a conflict or encounter a disagreement, make sure that you are able to resolve this conflict and find an agreement before the end of the day and before you hit the bed. In case conflicts are left unresolved, you are tempted to dwell on the argument you are having with your partner, coming up with worst-case scenarios in your head and widening the gap between you and your partner. Instead of working on resolving the problem, some couples allow anger and dwelling to kick in, making the problem even worse and unattended, which furthermore may create issues in communication as well. To avoid making your conflicts worse, try to resolve your arguments within the same day you entered a conflict with your partner. Clear communication – talking and listening on turns, while using logic and truth – is the best way of successfully resolving disagreements. If you are not able to resolve a conflict with the same day the conflict started, you may agree to give the argument a rest for a couple of days until you are able to figure out whether the fight you are having is worth fighting in the first place.

Stressors: Identification and Elimination

We already talked about the effects that external factors and outside stressors can leave on a couple, along the way affecting the harmony and dynamics of your relationship. Stressors may test your relationship to the furthest points where it may even jeopardize it – however, there is something you and your partner can do to prevent that and make your relationship stronger. This activity will help you connect with your partner, while learning how to appreciate each other's sensitivity and vulnerability to stressors. Moreover, this exercise should help you practice mutual support with your partner. Make sure that you are able to identify stressors and work on eliminating and diminishing external factors that are negatively affecting you, your partner, and your relationship. Stress factors should be identified and eliminated primarily because factors such as depression, illness, problems with finances or problems at work, can seriously damage your relationship. This is the case because we are sometimes stressed with numerous factors to the point where we are ready to vent our anger, insecurities, fear and other negative emotions, regardless of whether it is affecting the relationship with our partner. In case you are constantly stressed out, the chances are that you will release some of this tension on the cost of your partner's peace, which will push you into a conflict. Try to eliminate and identify stressors together with your partner to avoid negative case scenarios. It is perfectly fine to argue when there is a problem between you that needs to be resolved – however, venting due to the effects of stressors may only create a series of conflicts that are difficult to resolve until the real source of the problem is found and eliminated. So, for instance, if you are depressed, you need to talk to your partner about it to raise awareness on the fact that something is not quite right. Moreover, you may find an ally in your partner in eliminating and identifying the source of your depression. You may also choose to talk to a therapist towards finding a solution. In case you have problems at work, instead of relieving your stress in a way that would affect your partner and your relationship, you may talk to your partner and ask for advice, while letting your partner know that you have a problem that causing you stress. Any problem can be resolved when identified, while getting recognition, acceptance and understanding from your partner will make your relationship stronger.

No Excuse for a "Busy" Life

So, you and your partner are committed to numerous obligations and might need superb multitasking skills in order to take care of everything you need to do in a day. As a consequence, you have little room for spending some alone time with your partner. This type of case scenario can result in losing a connection you have with your partner, while emphasizing the lack of attention, appreciation and intimacy. If you are too busy and always too tired to spend some alone time with your partner, you may unintentionally convince your partner that you don't care enough to commit. Regardless of how busy and hectic your everyday schedule may be, you NEED to find some time for your partner in case you are motivated to keep your relationship alive and functioning. You can agree to spend more time together, while setting up the mandatory day off from all other commitments in order to dedicate yourself to each other. Make sure to schedule at least one mandatory date a week — the more, the better.

Cuddling

Cuddling, kissing, kissing, holding hands – physical intimacy needs to be practiced through touch and physical connection. Forget about stress, obligations and everything else that may act as a stressor or distraction and enjoy your partner's company. Relationships grow stronger with enhanced intimacy as romantic relationship simply need physical connection – and that is a pure fact. The lack of physical intimacy may make your partner believe that she/he is neglected, doesn't matter to you, while it may also convince your partner that you are losing interest in your relationship. This is a rather simple and rewarding activity for couples and it asks only for free time and free will. Lie or sit beside your partner, hug each other, kiss, hold hands, cuddle – be physically intimate and enjoy these moments of bliss as you are working on strengthening your relationship.

Chapter 4. Identifying Problems in the Relationship

A lot of couple's experience problems in their marriage or relationship and often times don't know where the problem originated from. Always lookout for these signs in your relationship. If your relationship experiences a couple of the issues that would be addressed below, then do well to work on those aspects in your relationship.

You don't spend enough time with your partner. You tend to do things for other people while not paying much attention to your spouse. You are more concerned about work or maybe you don't just see anything meaningful in spending time with your person.

• Solution - There is no doubt that you have to work to meet the needs of the family but it shouldn't be at the detriment of your relationship. While working to sustain the relationship, I also work to build the relationship. Dinner dates, vacations, weekend hangouts, evening walks, the movies or any other activities you both enjoy doing should be planned once in a while but consistently. During this period, you get to have privacy and you can discuss whatever issue it is you want to discuss. Spending quality time together also creates intimacy between you two and it makes your bond stronger and almost unbreakable.

You spend too much time together while neglecting other activities and leaving no space for personal growth

• Solution - it is important that you create time to spend together with your spouse but it doesn't have to affect other aspects of your life. Your children are there to look after (if there is any), your family (relatives), friends, your work, your personal growth, and some other affairs.

You find it hard to relate to or understand your partner's issues.

• Solution - this is actually very common among couples. Complaints like: "I don't know what else he wants", "after all I've done, she's still not getting it right" often pop up in relationships. Understanding your spouse is actually one of the easiest things to do. I will keep emphasizing effective communication and spending quality time together because all these things are interrelated, they work hand in hand and cannot be separated. Your relationship can only be better if you connect them and use them accordingly. When you have good communication with your partner and you take time out to spend together, as time goes on and you live together, you get to discover one hidden habit of your spouse almost every passing day. Through deep discussions and close watch, your partner's true self becomes more open and you begin to get a clearer picture of who your partner really is and what they want.

Either they or you often feel misunderstood. It's one thing for you to say or do something, it is another thing for your partner to understand what you have said the way you want them to understand.

• Solution - in most cases, these two don't connect. You say I e thing, your partner thinks another. This is actually normal because human minds are not structured exactly the same way. We may be staring at the same thing but have different opinions about that thing so don't feel bad when your spouse misunderstands you, rather, try to explain further and reemphasize your point.

You give away too much and get back too little.

• Solution - this issue as small as it seems, can be very critical and shouldn't be taken with levity. The relationship is all about given and take. When you give, get something in return. It is highly expected of you to give regularly to your person but if it becomes one-sided, it becomes tiring. The first thing you should do is talk to your partner about it and expect positive changes but if it reoccurs (constantly) and you can no longer bear with it, I think it's better to leave the relationship. Your generosity is gradually becoming abused and you will only get emotional stress in return.

You don't like or tolerate their vices. For instance, your partner is a drunk or a smoker, and you probably can't deal with it.

• Solution - communication comes in once more. Talk to your partner about it and try reaching an agreement. You could place them on conditions or agree on a certain number of bottles per day until they gradually get over it. If they seem addicted to it, it's your decision to make. If you can live with it, it's fine and if you can't, you know what to do dear. But whatever decision you make, consider your own health - physically, emotionally and mentally. Also, consider whether you can truly help them - that's if you wish to anyway.

Signs that You're Sabotaging Your Relationship

It is true that relationships have their own ups and downs and can be sometimes complicated but couples may be unaware that their own actions and inactions have contributed to the destruction of the relationship. Consciously or unconsciously, we do certain things that may have great adverse effects on our relationships. In most cases when problems arise, couples simply think that they are not good enough for each other or they cannot work things out without realizing they are the source of their own problem. Signs that your relationship is suffering from self-sabotage may include:

Negativity

You nurture the negative thought that your relationship is not going to last for a long period. This may come as a result of low self-esteem which makes you think you are not good enough for someone. This kind of thought makes it impossible for you to view a future together with your partner. When there is conflict in this type of relationship, you tend to give up easily and gets you thinking like "I knew we won't last long anyway"

Not Paying Attention

You are not always present even when you're together. This means, even when you're together with your partner, probably sitting next to each other, you are fully engrossed in some other things. It could be your phone or some office work or any other thing. You may not even be aware of your partner needs your attention at that moment

Bottling Up

You prefer to keep things to yourself rather than opening up to your person. How else do you expect your partner to know what you want or how to improve as your better half if you don't bother telling him your mind?

Lack of Trust

I call to trust the foundation of a solid relationship. A relationship without trust is nothing but a child's play. When you keep distrusting your partner, it gets tiring for the person. He or she get tired of explaining himself or herself over and over again and would just leave you to think and believe whatever you want to believe

Comparison

This is something that can really damage a relationship and most couples do it. Comparing your partner to your ex or your friends or his/her friends is a huge mistake to make. Why do you have to compare? You knew who your partner was before you decided to stick with him or her so you have to deal with it.

High expectations

Expecting too much from your partner will only kill the vibe even to do anything at all. You should know the ability and capability of your spouse, expecting from them more than they can give is totally out of it. This act only weakens the other person as they continue trying to keep up with your demands (that is if your partner is concerned anyway). Some partners will not even bother trying to impress you since they wouldn't want to do more than their ability and strength.

Another sign is that you feel like the victim in all your fights and make your spouse look like the bad one. Understand that one person in a two-people relationship cannot start a fight. You both contributed to it, so whenever you and your partner have a misunderstanding, don't try to play innocent. You are a part of it, you are both guilty. One person may have more blame than the other but two of you are certainly involved.

Chapter 5.   Common Relationship Pitfalls

Jealousy

Most people who experience jealousy in relationships mistake it for love. After all, you are only trying to protect your relationship, or are you? This is not just a fallacy but jealousy actually has the exact opposite effect of protecting your relationship. Jealousy is a destructive emotion that undermines trust in relationships. It feeds anxiety and drains all the joy from your relationship.

Jealousy is driven by insecurity and fear. When you are afraid of losing someone, you see potential threats everywhere. You get jealous of their relationship with their friends, family, or even siblings. You assume everyone is trying to get at your partner or break your relationship. The problem with jealousy is that, more often than not, it is based on irrational thoughts which lead to irrational behavior.

When jealousy takes hold, logic goes out the window and you become consumed with protecting what you consider your territory. Your behavior may get aggressive and, in some cases, even dangerous. Jealousy tends to stem from insecurities that have piled up over time until they start to evolve into the fear that you will lose your partner to someone else.

People with jealousy issues in their relationship tend to develop controlling tendencies. You want to control who your partner talks to, how they spend their time and how much time they spend with you. This kind of behavior makes the other person feel stifled and slowly starts to drive them away.

Anger

Have you ever unleashed a tirade against your partner for something as petty as where he left the toothpaste? Most couples will tell you that their fights started over small things that in the general scheme of things should not really matter. This is because when we start letting negative emotions fester, gradually small issues become big open wounds and before you know it you are full of rage and having angry outbursts at the drop of a hat.

Anger is a destructive emotion that makes you want to lash out and hurt your partner. When you feel aggrieved by your partner in some way you feel the need to hurt them in return. Anger can be one of the most destructive negative emotions in relationships. It can lead to aggressive behavior and fuel feelings of hatred and animosity.

Revenge

Wanting to get even is a natural human instinct. People feel the need to settle scores in order to heal from a grievance that was meted out on them. While this may work in sports and other competitions, revenge in relationships is destructive and usually the beginning of the end.

Retaliation only makes the situation worse because rather than trying to resolve the conflict you are giving in to your emotions and lashing out. While forgiveness is not easy, resorting to underhanded behavior or actions to get your partner back will not provide you with any solutions. Sometimes being the bigger person will save you a lot of additional heartache and stress.

When you feel vengeful or vindictive, step back from the situation and give yourself time. Most of the self-destructive decisions we make are made in haste. Ask yourself how the outcome of your revenge will benefit you. Consider what will happen if you go down that path.

Fear

Behind every dysfunctional relationship is an element of fear. Fear is a powerful emotion that affects how you think and act. When fear is driving you, your sole purpose comes down to neutralizing the perceived threat whether real or imaginary.

Fear takes away your independence and sense of self. Everything you do or even think is a reaction to what your partner does or says. This is why some people often get lost in relationships. Their personality changes depending on who they are in a relationship with. This kind of negative attachment puts pressure on your partner because your whole life revolves around them.

Poor Communication

The number one reason relationships breakdown is due to communication breakdown. Technology may have come very far but there is still no alternative to getting to communicating with your partner to know what they are feeling. When people cannot express themselves openly and freely in a relationship then it becomes impossible to be on the same page.

Real communication goes beyond just talking. It involves everything from tone of voice, body language, and other nonverbal cues. In fact, sometimes you can read much more into how someone is feeling through how they say things than the words that are coming out of their mouth. When the communication in your relationship is characterized by bickering, passive-aggressive behavior or even silent treatment. The distance between you and your partner grows greater every day.

Here are some common communication mistakes that couples make

a) Lying

Lying breaks, the trust in a relationship and leaves both parties feeling resentful and cheated. If you cannot be honest with your partner, then your relationship doesn't stand much of a chance anyway. Part of open communication is being able to talk about even the uncomfortable things, apologize when you need to, and own up to your mistakes.

b) Passive-aggressive behavior

Your partner does something that hurts you. Instead of telling them how you feel, you start treating them coldly or making snide remarks. Passive-aggressive behavior is usually a misguided attempt to cover up our true feelings. Instead of expressing how you feel, you try to vent frustration through sarcasm, stubbornness and sometimes refusing to communicate with your partner.

c) You text more than you talk

If you spend more time with your gadget than you do talking to your partner that is a major red flag. Mobile devices may be built to facilitate communication, however, in some cases, they can be the barrier to openly communicating with your partner.

d) You constantly interrupt each other

If you cannot listen to your partner long enough to let them finish their sentence, you are failing in the communication department. No matter how right you think you are, giving the other person time to express themselves shows that you respect and value their opinion. If you make a habit of constantly interrupting your partner, they may eventually get tired of trying to communicate with you and shut down.

e) Silent treatment

Avoidance is usually a coping mechanism that many people use when they do not want to confront a situation. In most cases, people with avoidance issues resort to silent treatment to express their frustration or displeasure. Instead of communicating with your partner, you may often find yourself avoiding conversations altogether.

Are you Playing Games?

Games may be fun for a while and may even provide you with some instant gratification. On a deeper level, people who feel the need to play mind games in their relationship are typically dealing with insecurities and lack the emotional maturity to have a healthy relationship. Most people who play games are usually trying to manipulate or take advantage of the other person.

Gaslighting

If you constantly find yourself manipulating the other person to make them doubt their own logic or question their motives you are gaslighting. Manipulators are excellent when it comes to gaslighting. They turn situations around and will do anything to transfer fault or blame to other people.

Projecting

Projecting is a common tool used by people with manipulative tendencies. They deflect and create a situation that their partner is so busy defending themselves that they do not notice what the other person is doing.

Guilt-tripping and Shaming

People who use your weaknesses or past against you are playing mind games to get you to do what they want. They will use any personal information they know about you to manipulate and control you. For instance, someone who knows you cheated in a past relationship or had a drug problem or any other mistake in your past will constantly bring it up to make a point.

Sending Mixed Messages

A little mystery adds a bit of romance to any relationship. However, if you are hot one minute and cold the next, you are keeping your partner on edge. Some people do this because they are unsure of their intentions or whether they are really interested in the relationship. Others send mixed messages in an attempt to hedge their bets so that in case the relationship does not work out they will not have too much to lose.

Withholding Affection

Do you often withhold intimacy or affection as a way of punishing your partner? Withholding affection is a common occurrence in many relationships. When you start using sex as a weapon, you undermine the intimacy in your relationship.

The Beginning of the End

Nobody wants their relationship to go up in flames but life does not always go according to the script we have in our head. The truth is relationships end. While some can be saved, some should end because they may be doing more harm than good.

For most people giving up on someone they love is usually a last resort. They hold on for as long as they can but holding on will only work if you know what the problem actually is. In most cases, you will find that the thing you most commonly fight about with your partner is not actually the main issue in your relationship.

Due to poor communication, avoidance, and lack of self-awareness, you may allow issues in your relationship to fester to such a point that you do not even remember what started the problem in the first place. In some cases, we delude ourselves into thinking that the problem will blow over with time and that the relationship will somehow fix itself.

The truth is before a relationship ends there are always signs that something is wrong. Even when you keep thinking I did not see this coming, there are always warning signs that point to the beginning of the end of a relationship. At their core relationships are more similar than they are different. No matter who you are with, there are problems that will sink your relationship slowly but surely.

Top Warning Signs that Your Relationship is in Trouble.

a) You no longer compromise.

If your relationship lately feels like a series of power struggles with you or your partner trying to win, this is an indication that you have both lost sight of the bigger picture. When your partner begins to feel like an adversary or competitor, it may be time to evaluate what is really going on in your relationship.

b) You are no longer interested

The more the distance between two people grows the less interested in their partner's lives they are. You no longer care about how your partner's day was or how he is feeling. You do not care what he does in his free time or who he does it with. This lack of interest shows you no longer care and that you are simply going through the motions.

c) Letting external stressors take a toll in your relationship

While stress is a fact of life, your partner should be the one person you can go to feel better after a long hard day. If you are no longer able to do that, it means that the support system in your relationship is broken down.

Chapter 6.   Components of a Healthy Relationship

Healthy relationships help us become confident, grounded and well-adjusted. But it takes work to have a healthy relationship with your partner. In healthy relationships, attachment issues are unheard of, and the partners are generally looking to help one another. The following are key pointers as to what a healthy relationship looks like.

- Partners bring each other up

Partners must have the mentality of helping each other out, not tearing each other down. Partners must always work as a team. When partners try to separate themselves, it gives room for resentment, and then they start to sabotage each other. The moment partners start working against each other, it's the start of the end, and they have minimal chance of ever salvaging what they have. Bringing each other up doesn't mean that you sacrifice your happiness. It simply means that you provide your support for the common good. Healthy partners will have no issues with being there for their partner for they recognize that they will eventually need help as well.

- Embracing each other's flaws

As human beings, we are flawed. We cannot didge that. We are flawed when we are single and we are still flawed when we get into relationships. In healthy relationships, partners don't call out each other for their perceived weaknesses, but rather, they simply embrace each other's flaws. This is not to mean that you shouldn't work to eliminate your weaknesses, but rather, it is an attempt to create a positive environment for the relationship, and it is far better when partners are always working to become the best version of themselves.

- You can be yourself

For some reason, some people think that it's okay to present themselves as someone that they are not. In most cases, these people are driven by insecurities. They seem to think that no one will appreciate their authentic selves, and they are forced to modify their persona. They are just cheating themselves. One might keep the façade only for so long. The worst thing you could ever do both to yourself and your partner is present yourself as someone you are not. In healthy relationships, it's okay to be yourself. It's totally okay to express your peculiar habits without catching judgment from your partner.

- Respect

In healthy relationships, partners have respect for one another. They understand that each one is an individual. They understand that they cannot control the beliefs of their partner. Partners won't fight each other over a difference of opinion or difference in belief. Having respect for your partner means that you are not inclined to bend them to your will. You recognize that they have free will and they have chosen to do as they wish. People in unhealthy relationships tend to experience unhealthy power shifts so that one partner wants to dictate the beliefs of the other.

- No room for codependency

Codependency means that partners rely on each other for their emotional and psychological needs. This kind of arrangement might be great in the beginning but it quickly grows old. Healthy relationships require that partners have separate lives. They need to have a life of their own that caters to a certain degree of their emotional and psychological needs. For instance, they need to have friends that they can rely on, and this will help them have an easy time during their tough times. Codependency denies partners a chance to establish roots with their friends. When problems arise, as they are bound to, the partner is in a tight spot, and such an arrangement accelerates they're falling out.

- Minding each other's needs

In healthy relationships, partners are not selfish, but rather they mind how their actions are going to affect their partner. Partners must be sensitive to each other's needs. Such an attitude promotes closeness between partners. Such an attitude ensures that partners are not driven to sabotage each other. The falling out usually comes after periods of not minding each other's needs. Problems start to crop up when one partner isn't mindful of how their actions affect the relationship.

- Appreciating one another

In healthy relationships, partners appreciate each other. This keeps their love going strong. When we talk about appreciating one another we mean that partners take their time to acknowledge each other's good deeds. Appreciating your partner doesn't always have to be a grand gesture. You don't necessarily have to fly your partner out to exotic places in order to show them that you appreciate their good deeds. Some of the simple ways to make your partner feel appreciated include writing love notes, buying flowers, and taking them out. After all, it's the thought that counts.

- Respect for each other's families

When two people come together to form a relationship, whether they like it or not, their families are involved as well. For that reason, both partners must have nothing but respect for each other's family. Neither of them should think that their family is better off, because such an attitude would encourage conflict. One of the things that shows partners are respectful of each other's family is through constant communication. They must reach out to their families and engage them sincerely in order to find out how they are doing.

- Intimacy

For a relationship to stand the test of time, the spark of love must be kept alive, or else it's going to be painful. The best way to keep this spark alive is through being intimate with one another. It is absolutely necessary that partners are intimate. In the absence of intimacy, it might point to a disturbing thought, the idea that one or both partners are getting intimate outside the relationship, and this would lead to conflict. Successful relationships take work. Partners must be willing to create time for intimacy and to explore their creative side so that it never gets boring.

- Honesty

In successful relationships, partners are not trying to deceive each other, but they are always telling the truth. It can be hard in some instances to tell the truth, especially when the repercussions are far heavy, but even then, you must earn to be honest. Being honest shows that you have respect for your partner. Being honest means that you care about your partner's feelings. You might have to face problems when you are honest with your partner but it doesn't compare with the kind of trouble you would be in as a result of not telling the truth.

- Have fun

One of the challenges that most relationships have is continuing to have fun. In the beginning, things are normally fine and dandy, and the fun is through the roof. But then time usually draws the partners apart so that they don't know how to have fun anymore. Healthy relationships don't allow it to get to that point. It is necessary for partners to expand their avenues for fun. For that reason, they have to be imaginative, or else the relationship will struggle. They have to have a growth mindset.

- Effective communication

Many studies have shown that poor communication ranks high up there – along with infidelity and finance squabbles – as the leading cause of divorce in America. Poor communication encourages the development of tension and disharmony in a relationship. In the long run, poor communication invites distrust and makes the partners go against one another. In order to have great communication in a relationship, the channels of communication must be kept open. Once a problem comes up, they need to face it, and not just bottle it up. The tendency to bottle up issues only makes the situation far worse because it reaches a point and the pent-up frustration erupts, precipitating a nasty fight.

- Making each other happy

It never stops. Partners must ensure that they are always making each other happy. Some people take this to mean they have to shell out a ton of money in order to make their partner happy. If you have the means, and there are no hard feelings, by heaven do that! But then making your partner happy is more about understanding the various things that put a smile on their face and making them smile a lot more. It means being sensitive to your partner's emotional evolution and making necessary adjustments.

- Trusting each other

In healthy relationships, people trust each other. They are not putting an eye on the back of their head as they hope to "catch" their partner doing something they should not. If partners cannot trust each other, the relationship is pretty much done for. It is extremely important that partners keep trusting each other. In order to ensure that you don't get it wrong, ensure you get it right in the beginning, which means screen your partner well. Be certain that you can trust them. If they are putting up a front, the situation cannot be helped, because cheats will always be cheats.

- Respecting each other's boundaries

Being in a relationship doesn't mean you are joined to your partner at the hip. There needs to be healthy boundaries so that you may respect each other's time. Even though you are in a relationship, understand that your partner must have another life, for instance, their professional life, in order that their life may be whole. When you trespass on their boundaries you make it hard for them to reach their milestones and it is an indication that you don't respect them. in a healthy relationship, partners respect each other's boundaries.

- Patience

In healthy relationships, partners have patience for one another. They are not hostile. They are not looking to drag one another by the hairs of their head for small mistakes. They are royally patient with one another. If one of them asks for a favor and receives a positive answer, they understand that their favor will be granted, and there's no need to make a fuss over it. They have learned to be patient with their partners and to always look onto the positive side. In unhealthy relationships, partners have a militant attitude toward each other. If they don't get their way there's going to be war.

- No jealousy

In healthy relationships, there's no jealousy. Partners don't look at each other with the green eye, agonizing about how the other person has it better than them. There's no possessiveness. In healthy relationships partners are supposed to support each other because they understand too well that the victory of either one will be shared between them. They are not caught up in a power struggle to try to see who will dominate the other. When jealousy enters a relationship, everything goes to hell, because it begins to taint the motive of every decision.

Chapter 7.   Ways to Keep the Fire Burning

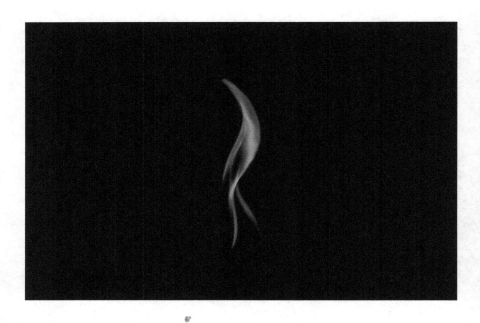

It is good to love your partner but never underestimate the place of God in your relationship especially in marriage. Marriage is a union that was instituted by God himself and the bible records that God himself is love. This explains that God is the only person who knows for sure what love truly represents.

Before you venture into a marriage relationship, communicate with God, during the relationship; stay with him and ask him to help you love correctly. This is a paramount part of a relationship a lot of people do not take rather seriously. So many relationships have collapsed as a result of this carelessness in actions. The bible explains a lot about God and love, even this was represented fully in how man and woman were created. This proves that no relationship survives the test of time without the place of God.

No relationship is perfect except one deeply rooted in God. It is pertinent to maintain a close relationship with God. Relationships are always surrounded with a lot of issues. Issues from sexual desires, health related issues and challenging circumstances would always come up. The only relationship that boasts of a good foundation is one that is connected to God. The best form of relationship is a union between both partners and God. An intimate relationship with God yields the much-desired relationship intimacy with your spouse. It gives peace of mind and brings forth joy unending.

The Place of Science and Consciousness

There is a science in every relationship. Unlike art, science is based on principles and theories. Any relationship that would amount to something good or useful, it must abide by these principles and theories. Every relationship is built on the premise of mutual understanding and connection. There would always be an external partner. A relationship is a two-dimensional structure with a three-dimensional outlook. This implies that asides being intimate with your partner, you must fully comprehend the place of consciousness and God. Absence of these factors shows that the relationship is headed for ruins.

Consciousness is required in a relationship. You have to be conscious of every part of the relationship. There are times when you become uncertain about the relationship. The uncertainty can as a result of certain changes that you may have perceived from your partner. Not too worry, change is constant and is bound to happen. The only thing that you need to concern yourself with is how to achieve a relationship that suits the both of you while also playing your role as a worthy partner.

Intimate relationship is not scandalous. Unfortunately, a lot of people tend to think that there are certain acceptable ways to give pleasure to your partner. Listen; there are no ways to that. As long as it doesn't affect your health or cause damage to your body part, indulge in it. Intimacy is important and even the scripture recognizes that sex is important especially in procreation.

Relationship of Sorts

The traditional form of relationship still thrives yet it has given room for other sorts of relationship. Inasmuch as these new types of relationships are not really applauded in the society, it doesn't take away the fact that they actually exist. Moreover, a lot of people are comfortable in a relationship that gives them peace and happiness. So, if it gives them such pleasure why disapprove of it?

The society frowns at a number of things as a result of cultural interference. One notable fact about this is that despite the stance the society has taken; a lot of other kinds of relationships are still encouraged today.

Today, in the relationship scene, we see a lot of other forms of relationship asides from the type that was prevalent in the society some years ago. We see relationship like homosexuals, lesbianism, multiple sex partners and all whatnots. This doesn't rule out the fact that what they share is also a relationship. The only difference is ideology and philosophy. Any form of union that involves people coming together with a mutual understanding is a relationship. It doesn't really have to mean sense to any other person but them.

In addition, there are cases of relationships where the partners do not even live together nor have sex together. And yes, this people are doing well and are satisfied. Why? They are bound by mutual understanding and agreement. They have come to terms with their realities are willing to stick to it. As long as they are comfortable with each other, the rest of the world has to deal with it. Also, some relationships have birthed their own kind of sexual intimacy. There are lots of available sexual styles that some partners prefer to indulge in to satisfy their sexual urges.

The underlying factor to any relationship is mutual understand and willingness. When two adults come together with an understanding to be together through thick and thin and despite the society's stance, this shows that they are willing to make it work. There are other cases where a 'couple' is made up of three persons. It may seem awkward but they have set up ways to make it work for them.

To maintain a healthy kind of nontraditional relationship, the partners have to come to a point of expressing their emotional needs. Been able to express yourself in a relationship can't be over-emphasized. A lot of things depend on it, there are certain areas that may not be comforting to a particular partner. Rather than keep quiet about it be honest in your emotions. Except you express your view, your partner may not really understand what you are going through. If there is anything you don't like in your partner, Speak up! Let him/her know about those stuffs. Another way to keep the nontraditional means of relationship going is to communicate effectively and appropriately. Communication is an integral part of any relationship. Even the nontraditional relationship partners understand the essentialities of this relationship type and as such they strive to be open to each other in communicating their needs.

By communicating, they attain a level of completely understanding each other's strengths and weaknesses along with their behavioral patterns. As long as this has been achieved, the partners find it difficult to fall out of love with each other.

Another integral aspect is practicing safe sex. Even in love, you must practice safety. Love doesn't expose you to risk factors that may mar your health or even cost you your life. As such, even whilst venturing into your kind of relationship ensure you practice safe sex. For partners who are asexual, it is important to protect your sexuality with so much vigor and zeal. More so, couple with multiple sex partners and other forms of couple must also strive to be safe by practicing safe sex. Inasmuch as the partners are in love with each other, they must also recognize the dangers of sexually transmitted infection and diseases as a result of carelessness.

Whatever form a relationship takes, it is important that the partners put into consideration a host of factors that are determinant in ensuring a successful relationship. For a relationship to work out well, both partners must be committed to it by playing their individual roles to ensure things take a good shape.

Chapter 8.   Relationship and Role of Mutual Blame

These are just a couple of instances of how individuals accuse each other. I'm certain you will think of more progressively about your own connections. What is important to remember about collective remorse is that it rarely works. It is typically in the form of disputes where a couple starts to indulge in a cycle of reciprocal responsibility. When this happens, a person begins to be more aggressive and angrier than at the beginning. This is letting you know you are at fault for something that says you are inept, to a fault, and to be frail in different regards. No man needs to be back in the corner and compelled to admit that he's wrong. When one's pride and reputation are concerned, it is important to prove the other person wrong, and then accuse him. In reality, despite realizing that they are to blame for something, the person would argue that they are to blame. For example, a man was presumably asked to buy a bottle of milk. Nonetheless, since they were in the midst of the fight, he undoubtedly denied that he had misunderstood and blamed her.

The substance of the relationship is to such an extent that everybody is to blame and, somehow or another, everybody prompts the issue. In other words, people in a relationship have an effect in hundreds of ways. Truth be told, it's far-fetched that anybody is completely to fault for a large number of the things that occur. Relating implies that there are associations between two individuals who share a past and a future together. Association doesn't imply that one partner prompted the other to occur. Every person is responsible for his or her own actions, independent and distinct from the other. Another example may be that "I stopped engaging because of your criticism" actually means "I feel like I want to stop when I hear the criticism." An old example is that "you gave me a headache." Why blame that on someone else?

At the end of the day, in a dispute, it is easier to consider solutions to settle the argument. Perhaps it's as easy as having a different way to phrase things. Communication is more than one individual talking. Or maybe, communication includes listening first, and afterward reacting in a non-protective way. For example, the use of the pronoun "I" while speaking is much preferable than the accusatory "You." Often, the use of the word "Why" as "Why Do You" is accusatory. It sounds a lot nicer to say, "I'm so upset that I was laid off that I want to blame everybody." Another way is to say, "I wish we could find a compromise that you'd consider reasonable." Choosing words is often necessary.

In a lifelong partnership, the goal would not be to win a point at the detriment of the other person, especially if you love the person. In tight connections, winning a contention can mean losing a companionship.

Seek answers rather than a fault.

Key Relationship Problems You Must Prevent

It is of course of the utmost importance to work on areas that can develop, construct and push your partnership to the next level. Around the same time, though, we must be mindful of the errors committed by other partners to undermine and ruin their marriages in irreparable ways.

The following are some things that you can remember and be cautious about in case you're attempting to make a solid, sound enduring and productive relationship:

Avoid Picking On Partner's Faults

No one gets a kick out of the chance to be judged, especially the one they love, so abstain from singling out your partner's shortcomings. You're not faultless yourself, so don't anticipate that your partner should be perfect either. Respect them for what they are, value them for their imperfection, and regard them for the certified greatness that falsehoods covered up underneath the outward appearance.

Avoid Complacency

Most marriages collapse simply because the pair is getting so complacent and relaxed inside the relationship. As human beings, we are hungry for novelty and diversity in our lives. At first, toward the start of the relationship, we experience a few new feelings and furthermore partake in occasions that produce anticipation, disarray and unusualness.

At the point when you've been dating somebody for some time, it's anything but difficult to totally overlook the reasons that initially produced the flash and energy in your relationship. At the point when you find that you are being messy and that your relationship is getting so exhausting, realize that at some point or another, one of you should plan something to spice it up, or, more than likely, the relationship is going to self-destruct, both intellectually and literally.

Stop Instant Gratification

It's exceptionally simple to get dependent on causing your partner to fulfill all the inward wishes and wants. Remember that despite the fact that you're seeing someone, still be a different individual with one beating heart and one brain. Dependence on your partner can well add to destitution, which can cause your partner to feel claustrophobic in your quality. Or maybe, consider being content with yourself when your partner isn't there. Additionally, work on satisfying your psychological, physical, good and material needs in a positive way, without requiring your partner to be there constantly.

At long last, understand that any relationship requires love and closeness the same amount as it requires a little partition and space. Thus, be mindful so as not to be snared.

Stop Carrying Old Baggage

By old baggage, I'm not talking about old bags that have been sitting in that wardrobe for quite a long time. Rather, I mean individuals, emotions, and discernments that trap you before and debilitate you from going on with your new relationship right now. Stay consistent with yourself by relinquishing the past and by thinking about your relationship with everything that is in you now.

Maintain a Strategic Distance from Unreasonable Assumptions

Get over in your mind that your partner can fix your relational troubles or confidence issues. Your partner is human; they can help you, yet you don't depend on them to help you with any inquiry that compromises you consistently. It's very intellectually debilitating and you will consume your partner's psychological vitality. You need to recall that they're, despite everything, battling with their very own issues at home, busy working, and wherever else they're experiencing life. Better believe it, love one another, and be there when your partner needs you most, however, don't cling to the bogus expectations that this relationship will offer you genuine satisfaction at any phase of your life.

Connections are not supernatural occurrence medicates that you can fly at any second, yet rather cherishing lifesavers that can help make your life change both less complex and progressively charming.

Quit Constraining Your Partner to Modify

It plays on the thought of accomplishment once more. You're not great, so don't anticipate that your companion should be immaculate either. Think back to your initial want and how you felt about your partner at that point. Do you criticize about any single thing you don't care for about them, or do you just appreciate them in light of what their identity resembled, an aggregate and magnificent heap of imperfections and everything? Your relationship has met up and you clearly praised each other's abilities and shortcomings. Prop this network up by attempting to be viable where it is powerless or proficient where it may be insufficient. Let yourself know, does the world truly need me to have another clone?

Value your partner for what their identity is and endeavor to try to accomplish the quality/shortcoming balance that is obvious in every single positive organization.

Until you can't help contradicting your companion, despite the fact that I show that my perspective is correct, is it worth causing my partner to feel awful about the way that they're off-base?

Let's all grow up and stop behaving like little girls. What is right and what is wrong is meaningless, as long as what is most important remains unchanged until it is finished and done.

Abstain from Creating Negative Anchor

This is the typical outcropping of the former mentioned point. At whatever point we experience a reliable and agonizing enthusiastic expression, all inside our present world is clearly associated with the passionate condition. It implies that in the event that you get back home from work feeling upset and pass that fury to your partner, at that point these sentiments of disappointment will gradually yet step by step keep on implanting themselves in your partner's essence. E.g., the next week you may be coming home from work feeling at the top of the planet, but the moment you see your wife you're beginning to feel insecure and furious, and you just can't understand why? That is proof that tells you that you have a detrimental magnet attached to your partner's body, and it is undoubtedly the most significant and most strong disruptive factor in the relationship of the 21st century. To stop this, really separate yourself from your partner at a second when you are having extraordinary emotions and attempt to be close to your partner while you are feeling happiness and expectation.

This methodology won't just douse the danger of having negative grapples, it will likewise offer ascent to the likelihood of creating positive relationship building stays.

After going through all these main steps, you will have the requisite techniques to develop and expand on your relationships in surprising ways. Try to be straightforward and reliable. Nothing is ever perfect, and nothing has ever been managed without a little devotion, readiness, and assurance. Keep the cycle fun, entertaining and rewarding, and your partnerships will undoubtedly witness the fruits of your success.

Chapter 9.   Things to Remember

Something that really gets a fight going is believing in stereotypes and accusing one another of their sex's stereotypical actions. "You always act like this! A person just can't win an argument against a woman." That, my friend, is asking for trouble. Nobody is the same and generalizing or assuming your partner's actions or intentions will throw gas on the fire. Here are some things to remember.

Life is Not a Movie

In movies, things always happen and turn out in a certain way. There's a massive fight between a couple who throw lamps at each other and yell until the neighbors report them. They say the most terrible things to each other and then it skips to another scene where they are all happy and in love again, holding each other tightly like nothing ever happened. That, my friends, never happens. Most arguments end with a week of silent treatment and someone ending up on a couch. In the movies, everyone can forgive and forget but in real life, she will never forgive you for sleeping with her sister. And he will never forgive you for breaking down his masculinity. There are lines that people cross in movies that should never be crossed in real life, and I wish more people could see that.

Even when a big-screen couple merely talks to one another, they say things that should never be said to one another. They lie, they cheat, they create unnecessary drama. I get that some people want more drama in their lives, but your relationship is not where you are supposed to get it from.

Forget everything that you have learned from TV and stay real. Don't make a big deal out of small things, don't think you can say anything and not feel the consequences later and above all else, don't expect things to go back to normal in the blink of an eye. This is real life, it's not a movie. People's emotions aren't faked so don't play with them or knock someone down for having them. They might not be as forgiving as fictional characters.

Not All Women Cry

 Just because a woman doesn't cry, that doesn't mean she doesn't care. Some women have better control over their emotions than most men. Just because a woman doesn't cry, it doesn't mean that you haven't hurt her feelings. You might have already broken her heart and she is too stubborn to show as much. Just because her cheeks aren't wet, that doesn't give you the right to say anything you want. You might not think it affects her, but it does. She's definitely crying on the inside.

Other women cry because of many things and it doesn't make her weak as I have formerly stated. It doesn't make her a wreck. She might be crying because she can't shoot you for all of the nasty things you've said. Remember that when you tell her she's a crybaby next time.

Don't assume that because she is a woman, she is just going to cry if you speak your mind either. Remember that all women don't handle things the same way and whether she cries or not, it doesn't mean she loves you any less or more. Some women just have a good grip on their emotions, while others' emotions are beasts, running around in the wild.

Yelling Does Not Mean They're Angry. They're Just Hurt.

Just like crying, people usually start yelling when they feel certain emotions. Luke has always tended to do this. He likes yelling to hide the fact that he is actually really hurt. Some people turn to tears, others to yelling and others to violence or silence. Take a more in-depth look into the action and analyze it from a different point of view. Don't try to match the volume of their outburst. If something sets them off, try a different approach. Sure, some people are angry when they yell, but sometimes, just sometimes, they try to cover up the hurt and fight back the tears with something else. It gives them something else to focus on.

Actions Have Consequences

Sometimes we do things without thinking. As children, we break rules because, in that moment, we don't care about the consequences. Sometimes, the punishments we got were worth it because we got to do what we desperately wanted to. As adults, we don't have that luxury anymore and our actions have more significant consequences that will stay with us forever. It's hard to think before you act, but sometimes it's a good idea just to take a moment and contemplate what you are about to do. Is telling him that he's useless around the house worth the consequences? Are you willing to lose a person so that you can get the satisfaction of hurting them? Remember that everything you do and say will cause a butterfly effect.

"Leave Me Alone" Actually Means "Leave me alone"

From personal experience, saying "leave me alone" usually means just that. Just give me some space to cool down before you get on my nerves again. I'm not claiming that Luke and I have a perfect relationship. Sometimes we still argue. Not as much or as wildly as we used to, but we still do and when that happens, Luke knows that when I tell him to leave me alone, I mean it. I hate when a person says, "When a woman wants one thing, she usually says the opposite." It's rubbish. If you are going to fuss over us while we told you to just leave us alone for a bit, the argument will get out of hand. When a man says, "leave me alone," women usually do so what is so hard about leaving a woman alone?

Flowers Don't Get You Out of the Dog House

When someone finds a man in the supermarket buying flowers, the first thought that pops into their heads is that this man messed up really bad and he has to make up for it. What sort of society do we live in? Women don't appreciate flowers anymore because we know that they're a man's strategy to get into our good books again. It doesn't work anymore. In fact, it just makes us even more angry that you think bribing us will make everything magically go away. Get your girl flowers because you want to treat her, not because you want to sleep in the same bed as her again. We appreciate communication much more than flowers in these situations. Especially since we know that men are more prone to avoid talking about their feelings than women.

No One Ever Forgets

The truth about human beings is that we never truly forget. We forgive, yes, but we never forget. Sometimes a person still gets a wave of sadness because someone said something 20 years ago. It's just the way people are. Don't fool yourself by thinking "forgive and forget" really exists. Only half of that does, and the other half is a lie we tell ourselves to make ourselves feel better about things we said to someone else. Deep down we know that we haven't forgotten anything ourselves. It all comes back to consequences. Whatever we do or say will stay with someone else forever and that is part of the consequences. They will always remember that one moment in history when they look at you and though it may fade in time and get buried over the years, in the first argument that surfaces again, it will resurrect itself.

It's unfair, it is. People change and they aren't the people they were all those years ago when they said it, but humans have a memory system. It's programmed into our minds. It's unfair but that's just life and the sooner people realize that, the sooner they will stop saying things that cause some severe damage. It's like losing a leg. You might be able to get a prosthetic but, in the end, you are still missing a leg. He might be able to forgive you for what you said to him, but the damage is already done.

CONCLUSION

It is common knowledge that successful and excellent communication enhances our everyday lives in terms of our relationships with people at work, with our families and with our partners or spouses. It is essential that all concerned parties strive to interact effectively in order to have a successful and lasting relationship and marriage.

Could I dig down deep enough to admit my hurts and my own needs? Where was I hurtful and distant with him? What was I asking of him that he had no capacity to give? What was I asking of myself that I was unable or unwilling to give? Diving into these questions helped me examine my own dark side, my own secrets and the lies I tell myself. Looking into your heart and shedding light on all the dark places lets you take a good look, and it's not always pretty. But, just sometimes, it's beautiful. I always had the vision of myself internally, as an over grown garden filled with wild flowers and weeds, all blooming at once. A beautiful mess.

CPSIA information can be obtained
at www.ICGtesting.com
Printed in the USA
LVHW081712270521
688665LV00015B/861

9 781802 343359